B-2 STEALTH BOMBERS

BY DENNY VON FINN

EPIC

BELLWETHER MEDIA · MINNEAPOLIS, MN

EPIC

EPIC BOOKS are no ordinary books. They burst with intense action, high-speed heroics, and shadows of the unknown. Are you ready for an Epic adventure?

This edition first published in 2013 by Bellwether Media, Inc.

No part of this publication may be reproduced in whole or in part without written permission of the publisher. For information regarding permission, write to Bellwether Media, Inc., Attention: Permissions Department, 5357 Penn Avenue South, Minneapolis, MN 55419.

Library of Congress Cataloging-in-Publication Data

Von Finn, Denny.
 B-2 Stealth Bombers / by Denny Von Finn.
   p. cm. – (Epic: military vehicles)
 Includes bibliographical references and index.
 Summary: "Engaging images accompany information about B-2 stealth bombers. The combination of high-interest subject matter and light text is intended for students in grades 2 through 7"–Provided by publisher.
 Audience: Grades 2-7.
 ISBN 978-1-60014-883-5 (hbk. : alk. paper)
 1. B-2 bomber–Juvenile literature. 2. Stealth aircraft–Juvenile literature. I. Title.
 UG1242.B6V66 2013
 358.4'283–dc23

                    2012032093

Printed in the United States of America, North Mankato, MN.

The photographs in this book are reproduced through the courtesy of the United States Department of Defense. A special thanks to Time & Life Pictures/Getty Images for contributing the photo on p. 7 and Ted Carlson/Fotodynamics for the photo on pp. 20-21.

TABLE OF CONTENTS

B-2 Stealth Bombers 4

Stealth, Crew, and Weapons 10

B-2 Missions 16

Glossary 22

To Learn More 23

Index 24

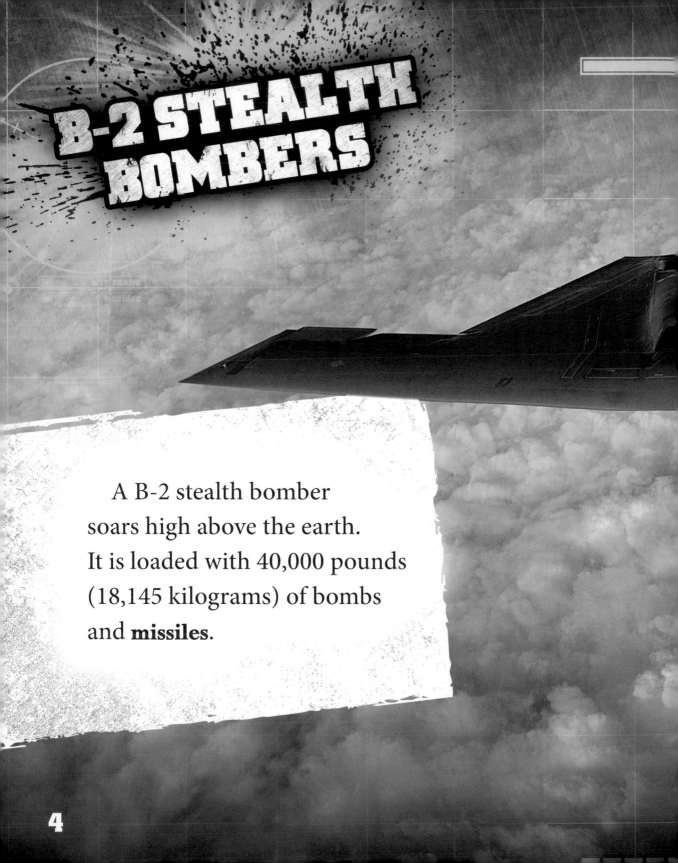

B-2 STEALTH BOMBERS

A B-2 stealth bomber soars high above the earth. It is loaded with 40,000 pounds (18,145 kilograms) of bombs and **missiles**.

Level

Latitude > 44° 49' 4" N

Longitude   5" E

5

Two U.S. Air Force pilots fly the B-2. They have flown for 15 hours without stopping. Their **mission** is only half over!

Stealth Bomber Fact

On long missions, one pilot can take a nap or eat a meal while the other pilot flies the B-2.

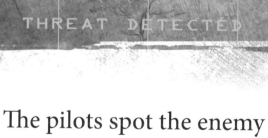

THREAT DETECTED

The pilots spot the enemy base. They drop bombs and turn for home. It is another successful mission!

9

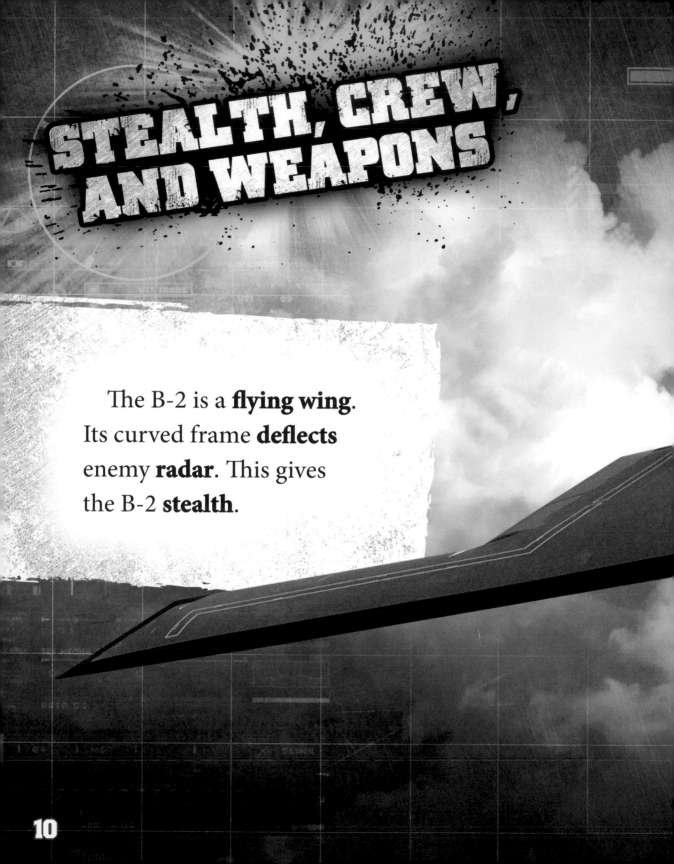

STEALTH, CREW, AND WEAPONS

The B-2 is a **flying wing**. Its curved frame **deflects** enemy **radar**. This gives the B-2 **stealth**.

Stealth Bomber Fact

The B-2 is covered in a special paint that helps hide it from enemy radar.

Four powerful engines
are hidden inside the B-2.
Enemy missiles cannot
sense the heat from
the engines.

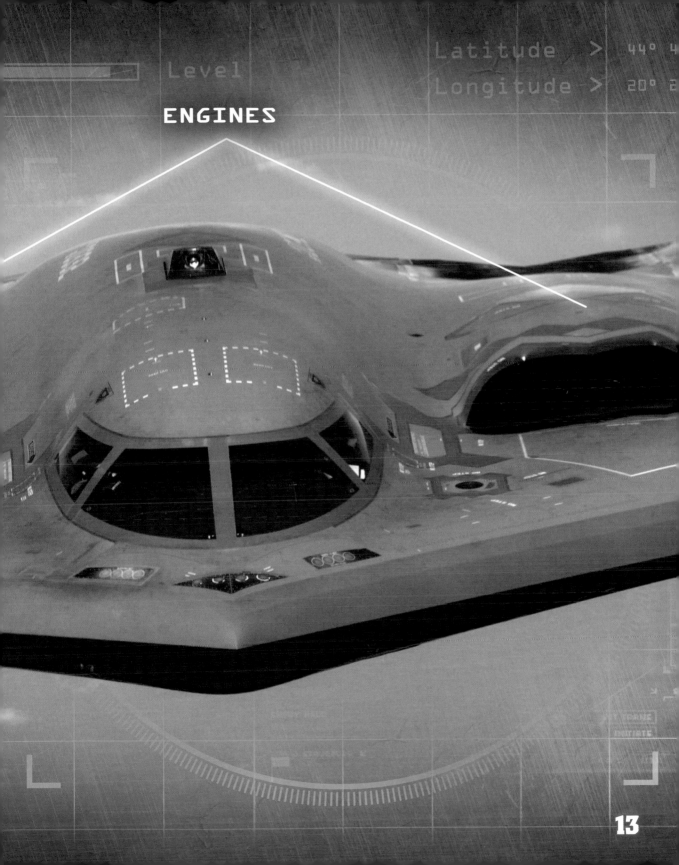

ENGINES

B-2 pilots sit inside the **cockpit**.
Bombs and missiles are in the
weapons bays behind them.

WEAPONS BAY

VEHICLE BREAKDOWN: B-2 STEALTH BOMBER

Used By:	U.S. Air Force
Entered Service:	1993
Length:	69 feet (21 meters)
Height:	17 feet (5.2 meters)
Wingspan:	172 feet (52 meters)
Maximum Takeoff Weight:	336,500 pounds (152,635 kilograms)
Top Speed:	over 600 miles (965 kilometers) per hour
Range:	6,900 miles (11,105 kilometers)
Ceiling:	50,000 feet (15,240 meters)
Crew:	2
Weapons:	bombs, missiles
Primary Mission:	air-to-ground attack

B-2 MISSIONS

Latitude
Longitude

Range |-|-|-|-|-|-|-|-|-|
0   50   100

The B-2 was built to attack quickly. It can fly to an enemy target and back home without being noticed.

Stealth Bomber Fact

The B-2 can fly as high as 50,000 feet (15,240 meters) and as low as 200 feet (61 meters) above the earth.

Range 0 50 100

Stealth Bomber Fact

The B-2 can be refueled in the air during long missions.

B-2 bombers reach speeds over 600 miles (965 kilometers) per hour. They can travel more than 6,900 miles (11,105 kilometers) without refueling.

The U.S. Air Force has 20 B-2 bombers. Their stealth, weapons, and **range** keep enemy forces everywhere on guard!

GLOSSARY

cockpit—the area inside an aircraft where the pilots sit

deflects—causes something to scatter

flying wing—an aircraft with fixed wings and no tail

missiles—explosives that are guided to a target

mission—a military task

radar—a system that uses radio waves to locate targets

range—the distance an aircraft can fly

stealth—an aircraft's ability to fly without being spotted by radar

weapons bays—the areas inside an aircraft where weapons are kept

TO LEARN MORE

At the Library

Cooke, Tim. *Bombers*. Mankato, Minn.: Smart Apple Media, 2012.

David, Jack. *B-2 Stealth Bombers*. Minneapolis, Minn.: Bellwether Media, 2007.

Hamilton, John. *B-2 Spirit Stealth Bomber*. Minneapolis, Minn.: ABDO Pub. Co., 2012.

On the Web

Learning more about B-2 stealth bombers is as easy as 1, 2, 3.

1. Go to www.factsurfer.com.

2. Enter "B-2 stealth bombers" into the search box.

3. Click the "Surf" button and you will see a list of related Web sites.

With factsurfer.com, finding more information is just a click away.

INDEX

bombs, 4, 8, 14, 15
cockpit, 14
engines, 12, 13
flying wing, 10
missiles, 4, 12, 14, 15
missions, 6, 7, 8, 15, 19
paint, 11
pilots, 6, 7, 8, 14
radar, 10, 11
range, 15, 19, 21
refueling, 19
speed, 15, 19
stealth, 10, 21
United States Air Force,
    6, 15, 21
weapons bays, 14